Views of Shropshire

Contents

Part 1 Introduction — 3
1. Diversity in Shropshire — 4
2. Ethnic Groups in Shropshire — 5

Part 2 Memories of Home — 7
1. Community: A Ghanaian perspective on community and belonging in Africa
   Hannah Adjepong — 8
2. At Times of Adversity: A story of hope and faith during the conflict between Azerbaijan and Armenia
   Irene Toone — 10
3. Colombia the Way I Remember it: A Colombian perspective on leaving one's home country and adjusting to life in Shropshire
   Claudia Doyle — 11
4. A Better Life: A Welsh Romany story about travelling around England and settling in Shropshire
   Harry Pence — 12
5. Young and Restless: Growing up in Japan during the Second World War and wanting to see the world
   Chieko Shove — 14
6. My Experience in Africa: A Polish story of living in Africa during the Second World War
   Janina Tobiasz — 15
7. I Have Seen Terrible Things: A Polish perspective on sharing bad memories with children
   Janina Remiarz — 16

Part 3 A Place to Live — 17
1. Meeting the Neighbours: A Peruvian story of moving to Shrewsbury and getting to know the neighbours
   Claudia Bullough — 18
2. The First Black Family in the Area: A Jamaican family buying their first home in Hadley
   Eulin Drummond — 19
3. The Camp: A Polish story about everyday living in the army barracks in Whitchurch
   Krystyna Tomczak — 20
4. Freedom: A Romany story about life in a purpose-built Traveller site in Telford
   Beverly Jones — 22
5. My First Memories: Life for a Polish family in army barracks in Higher Heath
   Lottie Jekiel — 23

Contents continued

Part 4 A Place to Work — 24

1. A Ghanaian Doctor's Journey: Training and working as a surgeon in the UK

   Samuel Adjepong — 25

2. The One-Stop Shop: An Indian family setting up in business in Newport

   Saroj Sharma — 26

3. Equal Treatment: A Ugandan Asian's reflection on working as a multi-lingual health care professional in Shropshire

   Pal Virdee — 27

4. Taking the Heat off the Situation: A Bangladeshi restaurant worker's experiences in Shrewsbury

   Sufu Amir — 28

Part 5 Community and Voluntary Work — 29

1. Setting Up Community Support Networks: A Ghanaian story

   Olivia Somuah — 30

2. The Family: A Bangladeshi opinion on family and community

   Torikot Ullah — 31

3. Making a Contribution: A Jamaican's thoughts on rural life and the importance of becoming part of the community

   Leon Murray — 32

4. Family Values: A Jamaican story of the relationship between father and son

   Verley Brissett — 33

Part 6 Becoming Part of the Community — 34

1. When We Came: A Jamaican experience of living in Hadley in the 60s and a reflection on changing times

   Merle Taylor — 35

2. A Slower Pace of Life: A Chilean perspective on fitting into Shrewsbury and feeling part of the community

   Alicia Randall — 36

3. Keeping the Connection: An El Salvadorian's view on raising mixed heritage children in Shropshire

   Consuela Avila — 37

4. Adapting to British Parenting Styles: A Ghanaian contrasts them with his home culture

   Zaglago Light — 38

Part 7 Future Hopes and Challenges — 39

1. Feeling Settled: A Japanese perspective on the differences between life in Japan and life in Shropshire

   Takeshi Kawai — 40

2. A Better Standard of Living: An Indian contemplates the changing quality of life in India and in Britain after spending forty years living here

   Rashpal Singh — 41

3. Open Spaces and Friendly Faces: A Taiwanese view of life in Shropshire and on education in Taiwan and Shropshire

   Mary Lu — 42

4. They Call Us Dirty Gypsies: A Romany perspective on stereotypes and misconceptions about Traveller/Gypsy people

   Julie Brown — 43

5. The Legacy We Will Leave Behind: A Polish view about the Polish migrants who settled in Shropshire after 1945

   Jadwiga Matecka — 44

6. Fading Identity: A Northern Irish perspective on identity and belonging

   Ann Baxendale — 45

Bridges – making global connections — 46

Part 1
Introduction

About this book

Imagine you had moved to Shropshire for the first time. Where might you live? Where might you work? What would help you to feel part of the community in which you now found yourself? Settling into rural and small-town life can present challenges for most outsiders. Poor access to transport, lack of amenities, few job opportunities and the problem of fitting into often small and close-knit communities are some of the issues new arrivals can face.

For the immigrants who settled in Shropshire in the second half of the last century, these challenges often took on an additional dimension. Some didn't know English, some found that the skills and qualifications which they brought from abroad were not recognised or were viewed as redundant. They didn't know how to get support and they might have been treated differently because of their backgrounds – their culture or race or religion.

"Views from Shropshire" explores the lives and experiences of thirty people who settled in this county from different parts of the world in the period since the Second World War. Their stories were gathered through interviews and workshops and recorded in their own words. This book is made up of extracts from those stories. It starts with some descriptions of the cultures and communities which people left behind and then tells of the difficulties and surprises they faced when they first came to Shropshire. It moves on to explore some of the diverse types of work they have engaged in and the parts some have played in their own community networks and in wider voluntary associations in the county. The final two sections recount how some of them have settled in Shropshire and what their views are of their and their families' future here.

These stories provide a fascinating glimpse into recent Shropshire history and into the richness of cultural diversity we have in the county.

Read, enjoy and admire!

Diversity in Shropshire

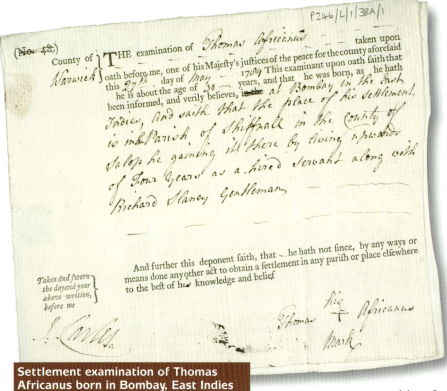

Settlement examination of Thomas Africanus born in Bombay, East Indies

Past

- As with all parts of the UK, Shropshire has seen immigration as part of its history from Romans, Vikings and Normans to present day refugees, economic migrants and students.

- Shropshire has remnants of its immigration history in buildings and historical archives, which document a black minority presence from 1704. Records at the Old Church Stoke Parish in Shropshire document the baptism of Charles Hector; aged ten from the West Indies. Other records document Thomas Africanus from the East Indies, who worked as a servant to Richard Slaney in 1785 (see picture above).

Present

- Information about diversity in the Shropshire County is shared across two unitary authorities: Shropshire and Telford and Wrekin.

- The 2001 Census shows Shropshire has a white majority, with ethnic minorities making up 1.2% of the population. This is significantly lower then the national average of 9.1% and the West Midlands regional figure of 11%. The largest ethnic groups are people from Chinese and 'other' backgrounds, which includes Traveller/Gypsy communities. Most ethnic groups have settled as individuals and families, with the exception of a small Bangladeshi community in Craven Arms.

- In Telford and Wrekin the picture is different. Ethnic minorities make up 5.2% of the population and have settled largely as communities. Telford and Wrekin is home to most of the established ethnic minority communities found in the UK, including Asian, Afro-Caribbean and the Polish communities who settled in the area in the 1940s, 50s, 60s and 70s. Telford has continued to attract new immigrant communities due to its industry, the availability of affordable housing and families joining their relatives in the area.

Future

- The largest growing ethnic minority group in the UK is predicted to be people of mixed-heritage backgrounds. Generally this tends to be people who have one parent from a White-British background and another parent from a different cultural or ethnic background.

- Many of the second-generation ethnic communities (people who are born in the UK but whose parents were born overseas) often move out of Shropshire in pursuit of professional opportunities and employment in other areas of the UK.

- Recently Shropshire has had an influx of Eastern Europeans due to EU expansion. It is difficult to predict whether these communities will settle here on a permanent basis.

Ethnic Groups in Shropshire

Eastern European communities

- Some of the Eastern European communities in Shropshire include people from Poland, Ukraine, and Slovenia.

- Most of the Polish communities settled in Shropshire after 1942, with the creation of the Polish Army hospital in Penley for war veterans and their families. The camp brought together Polish communities who had lived in Africa and Europe during the war. Although living conditions were basic they provided an opportunity for families to support each other and cope with many of their earlier experiences of the war.

- Some of the Polish communities stayed in Shropshire after the camp was closed and others moved to other parts of the UK and abroad. The established older community are small in number and have sought to preserve their history and experiences for future generations.

- information relating to the recent influx of Eastern European migrants is more difficult to come by. It is likely that the next census data will provide us with the most up to date information.

Chinese communities

- The Chinese community came to Shropshire in the 1980s and 1990s. The majority of first generation immigrants are students or people working in the restaurant industry,

- The main Chinese communities are mainly concentrated in Shrewsbury, Oswestry and Ludlow and some areas of Telford and Wrekin.

African communities

- The main African community came to Shropshire in the 1980s. Ghanaians are the largest community, and there are also people from Gambia, Sudan and Zimbabwe and other countries.

- In 2001 a group of African people set up the African Welfare Association to bring together the interests and needs of Africans living in Telford and Wrekin and Shropshire.

A Wellington Board School. On the left-hand side stands the teacher who is from an Asian background.

Japanese communities

- The Japanese community is mainly based in Telford and Wrekin because of Japanese factories that opened in the area in the 1980s. Most Japanese people settle in Shropshire for the length of their employment contract and return to Japan.

- Telford and Wrekin is home to 130 overseas companies employing 15,000 people, almost one fifth of the workforce. The highest number of employees are in Japanese operations closely followed by companies from France and the United States.

Asian communities

- The Asian community includes people from India, Pakistan and Bangladesh and has a variety of languages, cultures and religions.

- Indians are the largest majority in the Telford and Wrekin followed by the Pakistani Community, some of whom came as refugees after the Mirpuri earthquake. The Bangladeshi community are mainly concentrated in Craven Arms, although there are smaller communities based elsewhere. The Bangladeshi Welfare Association is the largest community network that spans across Telford and Wrekin and Shropshire.

- 2008 will mark fifty years of the Pakistani community in Regent Street, Wellington.

South American communities

- The South American community is relatively small and so has not been included in local statistics, although it is a community that has steadily grown over the years.

- Shrewsbury has the largest group of South Americans including people from Peru, Brazil, Argentina, Ecuador and Chile.

Traveller/Gypsy communities

- Telford has two authorised Traveller/Gypsy sites based in Lawely and Donnington. In Shropshire there are four sites based in Craven Arms, Cross Houses, Oswestry and Prees.

- The majority of Traveller and Romany communities based in Shropshire are thought to be people from Wales and Shropshire. Due to the transient nature of their Traveller/Romany lifestyles it is difficult to build a complete profile of these people in the area.

Welsh, Scottish and Irish communities

- The 2001 Census showed 6% of the County's residents were born in Wales, 1% in Scotland and less then 1% in Ireland.

- In some areas of Shropshire the presence of Welsh communities can be seen, with signs written in the Welsh language and translation facilities for people who speak Welsh as their first language.

Afro-Caribbean communities

- The Afro-Caribbean community are mainly based in Telford and Wrekin and arrived principally in the 1950s and 1960s. Many people came directly from the West Indies to areas like Wellington, which has the largest Jamaican community.

- Statistics suggest that the Afro-Caribbean population is an aging community with fewer young people born in Shropshire.

- Many of the experiences of the first generation of immigrants have been documented by the Black History Working Group.

Part 2
Memories of Home

If you were asked by someone from another country to describe your home, how would you start? Would you describe the building, the people, the community or the nation?

The accounts in this section give some insight into the places in the world which some people called home before they arrived in Shropshire. They also show that a home is more than where you live; it is about feelings, memories and experiences that give you a sense of belonging or a connection to the place where you grew up and the people among whom you lived. Sometimes, of course, these memories are tarnished by terrible events, as a consequence of wars, but then memories of families and their ideals become even more important.

Some of the stories here also show that Britain is not always people's first place of arrival. Sometimes, men and women travel around by choice or for work, but they may have left their original home and moved elsewhere for political or economic reasons before they came to Shropshire.

Community:
A Ghanaian perspective on community and belonging in Africa
by Hannah Adjepong.

Hannah Adjepong

Hannah Adjepong left Ghana in 1981 and lived in various parts of the UK before moving to Shropshire in 2005. Hannah worked as a midwife and is now retired. She now writes poetry in addition to her voluntary work with Bridges and the Visible Minority Development Council.

I think for most people, especially people from the ex-colonies we have a very romantic view about England that comes from films about picturesque villages, with people riding their bikes with baskets in front of the bike and everybody saying, 'Good morning'. When I came to this country I remember saying 'Good morning' and being totally ignored because, of course they do not know me, I am a total stranger. So this was a bit of a cultural shock for me because in my village everybody said good morning to each other and we asked about everything in the family, even if the chickens have laid any eggs [laughs].

Hannah's mother, picture taken in 1928

The village I come from is called Kransee in the Krachi district, Volta Region, Ghana. Like most African villages people have a close connection to each other, which comes from our culture. When a child is born, the village comes together for a naming ceremony to hear the name of the child and accept the child into the community. The child is not only the responsibility of the parent but every single person in the village and so that child grows up feeling secure. We haven't got what the British would call a 'stranger' in our culture. Most people will be trusted because of the way that Africans are raised, we have similar values. I grew up in a village where everybody was either a brother, sister, auntie, uncle, grandma or granddad. Every member of the family has a distinct name that reflects their role in the family. When you say *'mesekaa'* it means 'my father's younger brother'. *'Mesebrese'*, means 'my father's older brother'. And in the same way, my mother's sisters, *'minyibrese'* will be 'my mother's elder sister' and *'minyikaa'* is 'my mother's younger sister'.

Views from Shropshire

I do not know any time of when a child was in danger. The only time I can remember feeling fear is when a boy was abducted by a lorry driver because he had been throwing stones. The driver got angry and put the boy into the lorry and drove him twelve miles away from the village to the capital to Kete Krachi. I must have been about ten years at the time and I remember the whole village coming together and people crying and wailing, I had never seen grief like it. I remember the village chief and the elders getting together at the police station and gave the driver a good telling off because that is not the done thing; you do not take a child away from the home.

Looking back, I feel so privileged growing up in that society because I never felt alone and everyone had a place and a purpose in the community. And so, coming to England I have tried to keep my connection to community. To this day I always have people around to share a meal; if I should cook and eat I would not enjoy it. It is not part of my culture [laughs].

Hannah in her nursing days, 1971

At Times of Adversity:
A story of hope and faith during the conflict between Azerbaijan and Armenia by Irene Toone.

Irene Toone came to Shropshire in 1998 in connection with her work and is now settled in Cressage with her husband and three year old son. Here Irene explains her early memories of growing up in Azerbaijan during the collapse of the Soviet Union.

When I was growing up I had no sense of politics or religion because I was used to being around different types of people. I had friends who were Azerbaijanis, Armenians, Jewish, Ukrainians, you name it and we would meet each other, play together and share food. My own parents had come to Azerbaijan from elsewhere; my mother from Belarus and my father from Russia. My family are Christian, which makes us very different from the majority Muslim population but it had never been a problem until the conflict broke out.

The conflict started with the collapse of the Soviet Union. I remember watching news reports of Armenians invading the country and subsequent riots and conflicts breaking out. Many of our close family friends had left the country and moved to places like Russia, Ukraine, Israel and Germany and for those of us who were left we felt vulnerable.

Everything about our life had changed, all the normal day-to-day routines I had been accustomed to as a child. My parents kept me home from school and the only way I could contact friends and family was by telephone. We heard of fires being set to mosques and churches and refugees pouring into the city, many of them displaced and looking for a place to stay. I remember sitting in our flat and listening as refugees attempted to break into the flat opposite, only kilometres away. It was a nightmare and there was nothing we could do. There was so much suspicion and fear at that point we did not know who to trust. My family felt particularly vulnerable because of our faith. We thought people might associate us with Armenians because they are also Christian; sadly some people do not make a distinction.

I think in times of adversity people find their own way of getting through. It is almost as though you are always looking for someone or something to give you help or to give you sanity. Fortunately I have very close friends and family which helped. I went to Bible College regularly, which was useful because it brought together people who had similar experiences and helped us reconnect to a community and feel safe again. I think my experience helped make me a stronger person and I think that whatever you go through in life, you have to face up to it and become a better person. That is my message to everyone, stay strong.

Colombia the way I Remember it:
A Colombian perspective on leaving one's home country and adjusting to life in Shropshire by Claudia Doyle.

Claudia Doyle left Colombia in 1985 and lived in London before moving with her English husband to Shropshire in 2002. Claudia worked as a kindergarten teacher in her home country and now is studying to work as a Nursery Nurse in Shrewsbury.

Even though Colombia has a lot of poverty, we did not see that so much growing up. Although we heard stories of people stealing food, we knew it was about survival. Everyone has to eat and this is the only way they can survive because Colombia does not have a welfare system and some areas are very poor.

I grew up in Bogota in Colombia, although we travelled around a lot with my father's senior position in the police force. I had a lovely childhood and I can remember playing outside after dark until we were called indoors by our parents. We had lots of parks and space to play basketball, volleyball and spin the bottle and did all the normal things that children do.

I did all my schooling in Colombia and worked there as a kindergarten teacher. I owned three kindergarten clubs there which were sold after I got married. In Colombia, education is very different than over here. If you do not pass a subject you are not allowed to progress onto the next year. At school we have to learn English, although it is very different from how it is spoken here. When I first came here I remember trying to communicate with the four or five words I knew and I realised because of my accent people could not understand me. It was a complete nightmare. I remember asking for directions in London and having to mime words I could not pronounce and we were jumping about like monkeys.

I lived in London as a student and worked as a waitress and then came to Shrewsbury to waitress at my friend's restaurant. The pay was a lot less here and even though I am not qualified to work as a teacher here, I love it. Shrewsbury is my home away from home.

A Better Life:
A Welsh Romany story about travelling around England and settling in Shropshire by Harry Pence.

Harry Pence[1] was born in Wales and has travelled all over the UK before settling in Donnington, where he has lived with his family for over thirty years. Here Harry shares his memories of travelling and how upbringing in his times was different from that of Romany children growing up today.

We had a better life then, everything was quieter and we had no bother. We would travel in horse-drawn wagons passing from village to village in every part of England. We could never get sick of one place because we did not stay there long enough. At spring we would work in farms in Worcester, Evesham and Hereford picking apples, potatoes and then come back the following year to do the same thing. In every place we would meet travellers and old friends who we had not seen for years and we would spend a week together before going our separate ways. Everyone made you feel welcome and they were glad to see you.

We had a slower life too because everyone used to get about on horse-drawn wagons, you had time to stop and take things in and appreciate the beauty around you. The police would give us advice and say 'Stop at such-a-such road' and then 'Go to this area' so we would have fresh parts for the horses to graze and have a good drink of water. We had no electricity or running taps the way we do now and we used to fetch water in chrome cans and heat it on stick fires. We didn't have televisions either, but we did have a wireless with a big battery and we used to knock a peg in the ground to get the aerial up and listen [laughs]. I used to play the melodeon and we would get together and sing and dance. We put the gramophone on

Picture of a traveller encampment on the Whitcliffe, Ludlow c.1890

and played records and the boys and girls would step dance and enjoy themselves. If we went to Appleby[2] we would go as families and as a young boy, I would love seeing the horses, carts and wagons and the old men singing in the pub and sometimes I would mind their horses for them, in return for crisps or pop.

These days everyone is in a rush to get everywhere. People have motors and you can get from one end of the country to the next in a few hours and maybe blow the horn if you see someone you know along the way. People do not stop or talk the way they used but times are different now. Children have different pressures than we did, like going to school, peer pressure and drugs. We did not have that in my day. Some of our children are moving into houses too, which is a shame really because the lifestyle is fading away but I suppose we have been lucky with our own children and so we have nothing to worry about.

Shropshire is a home for us now, but who knows? In the future we might just take up travelling and go somewhere different!

[1] Pseudonym chosen by the interviewee
[2] Appleby in Yorkshire is the site of the famous Traveller horse fair.

Young and Restless:
Growing up in Japan during the Second World War and wanting to see the world by Chieko Shove.

Chieko Shove left Japan in the 1960s and lived in different parts of Asia and Australia before settling down with her English husband here in Shropshire. Here Chieko reflects on her upbringing in Japan and what inspired her to travel.

The Japan I grew up in is very different to how it is today. There were no skyscrapers or high rise buildings, it was actually very poor, as you would expect, because we had just survived the atom bomb.

I spent most of my childhood in the countryside and moved to Tokyo to go to university. In Tokyo most people lived in slums then and the standard of living was very, very poor. In spite of this, Tokyo was also a very dynamic place for young people because, for the first time, people of my generation started to get more active in national politics.

I joined the Student Union at university and I remember going on demonstrations through the night and talking about politics, everything from socialism to capitalism. We were not radical, because we had no intentions of overthrowing the government. We just wanted our voices to be heard and to consider different ways of doing things. It was an exciting time for all of us, but of course it did not last, because the national focus was channelled into modernising for the Tokyo Olympics in 1964.

After the Student Union died, I started to feel restless. I wanted to go out and see the world and meet different types of people. I did not have much money at the time, so I brought a single ticket and headed off to Singapore, Australia and then Britain. I had no plan of what I wanted to do or even where I wanted to go. I just followed my instinct and learnt as I went along. I think as long as you smile, talk and share you can make friends with everyone, which I have in different parts of the world.

It is only when I met my second husband that I finally put my roots down and stayed in one place. I suppose this has a lot to do with my age; the older you get the more you need familiarity and comfort as opposed to excitement and change.

My Experience in Africa:
A Polish story of living in Africa during the Second World War by Janina Tobiasz.

Janina Tobiasz at four years old

Janina Tobiasz came to Tilstock, Shropshire in 1948. Janina left Poland in 1938 as a Prisoner of War and spent two years in Siberia before moving around various parts of the Middle East and Africa. Here Janina talks about her memories of living in Uganda and her first bit of normality after witnessing some of the horrors of war.

We lived in huts made up of bamboo sticks and on the roof we had mud and grass, to keep the hut cool. It was odd not having a proper ceiling, because you would have thought the grass roof would cave in, but it never did. After six o'clock we were given mosquito nets to cover ourselves when we slept. It used to get very dark quickly and at night you would worry that lizards would drop from the walls. The window of the hut was made out of wooden shutters so you could take them off and make other things. We made legs for a table and I would sit there and do my homework or write a letter to my father, who at the time was building railways in Egypt.

I stayed in Africa for six years. I went to High School there and we would study every blooming subject. You could never study one subject in depth because they wanted you to know a little bit of everything. It was a good school, but a lot of the teachers were tradesmen so even though they were highly knowledgeable they did not know how to share their knowledge. Because we lived in a British protectorate, access to food and goods were rationed and sometimes it made life difficult for us. If we ever had a disagreement with the bosses they would confiscate our pocket money. Once my mother was suffering terribly from malaria and she was instructed by the boss, a Polish man, to make flowerbeds on the site. My mother had only just come out from hospital and so she needed to rest but when she protested, he took her pocket money away, money we needed to buy stamps so we could write to our father.

We had difficult times but we also had happy memories. For most of us Africa was the first bit of normality we had during the War. We had a Polish church and a Polish school and Girl Guide groups. So even though the conditions were not ideal for most of us this was our first bit of normality.

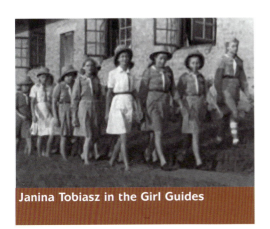

Janina Tobiasz in the Girl Guides

I Have Seen Terrible Things:
A Polish perspective on sharing bad memories with children by Janina Remiarz.

Janina Remiarz was born in Poland in 1929 and lived in Redditch before moving to Shropshire with her husband in 1960. Janina Remiarz left Poland as a Prisoner of War and worked in labour camps in Siberia before being taken to the Middle East and Africa. Here Janina talks about sharing some of her most painful experiences with her children.

I was twelve at the time and I remember my mother being given a sack and instructed to pack everything from food, hammers and spades. My mother must have panicked; perhaps because she thought we would be digging our own graves or something. She literally froze still with terror. The Russian army officer took the sack from her hand and proceeded to pack everything into it from meat, flour and sugar. We did not know where we were going to or how long we would be gone for. We were taken on horse drawn sledges and loaded onto cattle wagons and taken away to Siberia. We were all packed in the wagons, men, women and children. I remember sitting on the train and watching as a family friend was separated from her disabled child. She was literally pushed on the train while her child was left standing on the platform because they had assumed by looking at her, that she was not strong enough to work, for all we know she could have been killed by a passing train.

I have seen some terrible things happen with my own eyes. I remember sitting on the train and seeing prisoners being let out on release and literally dropping to their death because they were so weak and hungry they could not cope with the extreme cold. I watched their fellow prisoners taking clothes from the dead bodies before dropping to their own death only a few kilometres away. I also remember sitting on the train next to a girl on an overnight journey, only to wake up and find her dead by my side. I try not to talk too much about my past, especially with my children, but occasionally things come up when we are watching TV. If I go too much into it, my children will say "No I do not want to listen" because it is all so depressing for them, but maybe someday I will write it all down for them to read about it instead.

Part 3
A Place to Live

Many of us will have moved home at least once in our lifetime and will remember the mixed feelings of excitement and apprehension as we moved into a new neighbourhood. But reading the stories here may encourage us to imagine what it is like to move into an area when you don't know the language and also to imagine adjusting to cultures and values quite different from your own.

Meeting the Neighbours:
A Peruvian story of moving to Shrewsbury and getting to know the neighbours by Claudia Bullough.

Claudia Bullough moved to Shropshire in 1993 with her English husband and her two sons. Here Claudia talks about the first time she moved into her neighbourhood in Shrewsbury.

Before I came to England I remember asking my husband 'Do people look like me in England?' because I assumed everyone would have blue eyes, pale skin and blond hair. I had never been away from home before and although I was excited I was also a little apprehensive. I had so many questions, 'Can people speak Spanish?', 'Are people Catholic?' because all aspects of life in Peru are centred on the church from births, deaths and marriages. In fact, Paul and I were married in a Catholic Church in Peru, where we met almost twenty years ago. I worked at the British School in Lima and Paul worked as an English Language teacher. We spent most of our early married life travelling and working in Peru and Chile. It is difficult to get a stable job in Peru because most companies operate on short term contracts and opportunities are limited, particularly for the poor. I come from a middle class family which meant I had a good standard of education, although most Peruvians cannot afford to send their children away to universities or even buy their own home.

Eventually we made the decision to come to England. We lived in Twickenham in London, which is where Paul's parents live. I liked it there; there were a lot of English people who could speak Spanish so it was easy to communicate and get around. It was only when we came to Shrewsbury that I struggled because I could not speak much English. Paul always encouraged me to speak whatever little English I could, he'd say 'keep talking, get used to speaking and people will find a way of understanding'. When we first moved to Shrewsbury, Paul wrote out a little script so I could introduce myself to my neighbours. I remember taking my two young boys and knocking on my neighbour's door. I literally read my script word for word, 'Good morning I am Claudia, I am your new neighbour and these are my sons Andrew and Stephen'. I think they must have been a little overawed at first but they soon warmed to me and invited me over for tea the next day. Of course I did not realise 'tea' is an evening meal, so it was quite a surprise when I got there [laughs]. I have found most English people are quite reserved and shy until you introduce yourself and then they are very receptive and accepting. This is so different from Peru where people are very forthcoming and would not think twice about inviting themselves over or organising a surprise party for your birthday. I like this aspect of my culture and I have tried to keep it with me, even here in Shropshire.

The First Black Family in the Area:
A Jamaican family buying their first home in Hadley by Eulin Drummond.

Eulin Drummond came to Hadley from Jamaica with her family in 1962. Here Eulin talks about her experience of buying her first home in Hadley.

Eulin Drummond and her father

I was one of the first black families in the area and in those days coloured people could not get housing the way that they can today. It was awful finding a house for sale and being turned away or worse still not having the door opened at all. We were luckier then most because we had met a friendly English couple, who wanted to help us settle down. They suggested if we saw a house we liked they would buy it and sell it back to us. Of course we were touched by their generosity but we decided to decline their offer, I guess this is something we had to do by ourselves.

Months later, my husband went to the estate agents and saw a house for auction in Hadley. It was lovely house, perfect for our family, but it was out of our price range. We put in an offer and decided to wait and see what happened. On the day of the auction my husband fell ill and I was devastated because I knew at six o'clock that very same day, the auction would be over, along with our dream of having our own home.

The next morning we received a surprise visit from the estate agent to inform us that our offer had been accepted. I can remember jumping with excitement and running upstairs to pack my belongings in preparation for the move. However, when we arrived at the house we realised that not everyone shared our excitement. Most of our neighbours had sold their house and moved out of the area, perhaps because they did not want a black family living near them. As time went on people warmed to us and accepted us as part of the community. I think it helped that both my husband and I are involved in the Salvation Army because people can see we are genuine, God-fearing people. Now we have many different nationalities living in this neighbourhood, which shows how times have changed.

The Camp:
A Polish story about everyday living in the army barracks in Whitchurch by Krystyna Tomczak.

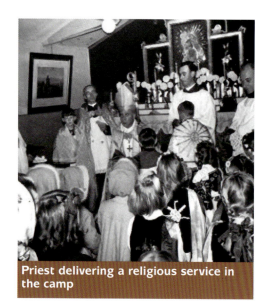
Priest delivering a religious service in the camp

Krystyna Tomczak was born in Trani, Italy and came to Shropshire only a few months old in 1946. Krystyna's parents were Prisoners of War and had been taken from Poland to Siberia, where they had been forced to work in labour camps during the Second World War. Here Krystyna talks about her early childhood memories of growing up in an army camp in Tilstock.

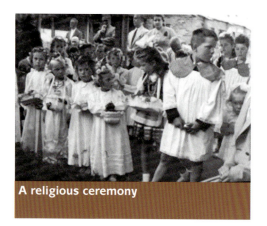
A religious ceremony

We had no option of going back to Poland because we had nothing to return to. Our homes had been destroyed by the Russian and German occupation; those who did go back were never seen or heard of again.

The camp in Tilstock meant everything to us; it was our Poland away from Poland. The camp had all aspects of Polish culture, traditions and festivals. We had a church, where we would take part in processions and celebrations and also a Polish school, where the priest would come and teach us religious education. I remember we were never allowed to put our hands up in class and I could never quite understand why, until later we had learnt the priest had been taken by the Nazis and had part of his nose cut off. Understandably, the raised hands reminded him of the Nazi salute, but of course we did not realise that because we were so young.

We went to Polish school until the age of seven when we were enrolled into a local village school in Tilstock. A whole busload of Polish children was transported from the camp to the school. The school had one head teacher and a few teachers. They did not have the support of teaching assistants or language support and they had to do the best they could with the limited resources available.

Children at the Polish School, Penley

It was difficult adjusting to school life at first. The school taught very differently from the camp, where we would learn by remembering and repeating information. At school you did not only have to remember but understand and apply your knowledge, for some it was difficult. Fortunately, I picked up English quickly and so I was heavily relied on in the camp. People would come to me to fill in forms or go to the doctors and so I would be the first to know everything.

I was very lucky because I went on to be educated and to become a teacher. Although at the time, opportunities for the Polish community were limited to manual jobs in farms or factories. It was tragic to see people who had been professionals in their home countries doing menial jobs. I think education was really our only way out from that situation. That is why I say to my children, 'whatever you learn you will never lose'. You just never know when you need that information you have learnt.

Children playing at the Tilstock village school. Many of the children in this picture are from Polish backgrounds.

Freedom:
A Romany story about life in a purpose-built Traveller site in Telford by Beverly Jones.

Beverly Jones[3] was born in Much Wenlock and has travelled and lived in different parts of the UK before settling in a purpose-built Traveller site in Donnington in 1974.

Well what it means to be a Traveller is freedom. I think if you have not got your freedom then even all of the wealth and possessions in the world are no good for you. Freedom is about being able to go wherever you like; as long as you do not hurt anyone or interfere with the lives of others I think you should be able to roam as much as you like. I don't feel free at the moment to be honest. We have been put into this Traveller site, 30ft by 30ft, and this is where we have to stay. We do not have the option of travelling anymore because people complain about us wherever we go.

If I was given a house, I would not know what to do with it. I like being out in the fresh open air. When I get up in the morning, the first thing I want to do is go outside. I take my grandchildren out and they'll say 'Come on granny, let's go for a nature walk' and so we go with sticks and poke the dirt looking for frogs or hedgehogs. I love nature, I don't know what brings it out of me, but that is how I am. Even now, I could take you back to all the routes and stopping places my father went to in wartime and even my grandfather. I always point them out to my grandchildren and tell them how we used to stop on our travels to let the animals rest and how we collected water on foot.

You know there are so many beautiful places to see in Britain, Scotland and Wales and so many parts of the country I have yet to see. I can't believe that some people in this country would rather jump in a plane and travel to another part of the world to sit in a bar, probably the exact same thing they do over here, rather then experiencing the seaside and all the lovely places we have here.

[3] Pseudonym chosen by the interviewee

My First Memories:
Life for a Polish family in army barracks in Higher Heath by Lottie Jekiel.

Lottie Jekiel left Tanganyika and came to Britain at the age of two and a half in 1947. Her mother had been a Prisoner of War and had been separated from her father in Siberia, where he was never seen or heard from again. Lottie's first experience of Shropshire is in Higher Heath were she lived for ten years before moving to Wellington with her mother and step-father in 1956.

We were billeted in a hut made out of bricks in Higher Heath, where I lived with my grandmother and occasionally with my mother, who had remarried shortly after we came. My grandmother was quite a character; everyone loved her and would come to her. She would buy wool and knit jumpers and scarves for the children and cook for them. Her speciality was belly pork dripping with onions and stuffing that she would serve with fresh bread. When I came back from school, I would go straight to the kitchenette with half a dozen friends just to eat it. My grandmother made her own oven, using clay, bricks and stones that she had collected from the woods. She would light the oven and when it was really hot, she would put her baking tins in, along with everyone else's of course. As soon as people heard about my grandmother's creation everyone wanted to use it.

I split my time between my grandmother's house and my mother who rented a room in a big mansion near the hospital where she worked. When I went over, she would have to partition the room using blankets because it was just one big living space, but it was still comfortable. I have some very happy memories of the camp. We had a community there with a church and school. We had plays, dances and processions and competitions too, which would enable us to meet people in the wider community.

Occasionally we would overhear our parents talking about the war, but it would never feel real to us because we could not understand. It is only as I am getting older that I am starting to realise how important these memories are.

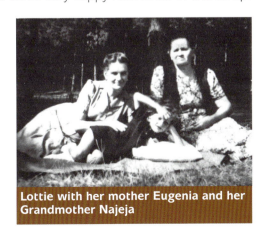

Lottie with her mother Eugenia and her Grandmother Najeja

Part 4
A Place to Work

Work is more than earning a living. It may provide us with self-esteem and confidence. It also offers a chance to help support families left behind and to give back to the communities that we live in. The accounts in this section provide an insight into the working lives of some of the people who have settled here. They include professionals, independent businessmen and women, some employees in large enterprises and some in small enterprises, for instance a restaurant.

At the time when most of our informants came to Shropshire, they had one great advantage. Work was available and there were big employers such as GKN Sankey that were ready to take on new employees. At the present time, new arrivals to Shropshire may face greater difficulty in finding worthwhile work.

A Ghanaian Doctor's Journey:
Training and working as a surgeon in the UK by Samuel Adjepong.

Samuel Adjepong came to Britain in 1980 to practice medicine and has lived in various parts of the UK and the Gulf before settling in Telford with his family. Samuel now works as a surgeon at the Princess Royal Hospital.

If I had been a surgeon in Ghana, my life would have been very different. Perhaps I would have been a professor or in charge of a hospital [laughs]. It is difficult to say really because my colleagues are scattered all over the world but those who have stayed in Ghana have a high level of responsibility, so it is likely I would have had the same.

My main motivation for coming to the UK was initially to train as a surgeon. I did the first part of my medical training at the University of Ghana in Accra and then I came here to complete the second part. In Ghana doctors train abroad depending on their area of specialism, either to Europe, America or Canada. America is a good place for medicine and Canada for paediatrics but Britain is the best for surgery. As many British surgeons are affiliated to universities in Ghana, it enables doctors to come here and train as they work. I came with eight other surgeons in December 1980. It was not too much of an adjustment to come here, because we speak the same language in addition to other local dialects, although some aspects of the culture are different. In Ghana we assumed most people in England would be Christian, because the English of course, brought Christianity to Ghana. So it was quite a shock to come to England and find churches empty or being sold and to find most people in the medical profession followed no faith.

The training system I undertook when I came here is very different to how it is today. This is because the training criterion is always changing and being updated. When I came back from working in Saudi Arabia, the training system had changed to such an extent that in order to get to the level I was before I had left, I would need to retrain again. So I decided to move into staff grade surgery, which is what I do now. I came to Telford because there was an opportunity to work at the Princess Royal Hospital here and I have been here ever since. I like it here, I have good job satisfaction and I work with a good team. I think that there will always be part of me that will want to return home to Ghana, but for now this is my home.

The One-Stop Shop:
An Indian family setting up in business in Newport by Saroj Sharma.

Saroj Sharma left India in 1954 at the age of six to join her father, who had been living and working in Smethwick. Saroj Sharma came to live in Shropshire in 1979 and now lives in Telford and works as a Counsellor.

We were travelling back from North Wales to Wolverhampton. We had been on holiday, and we decided to stop off in Newport for some refreshments. We parked the car and went to the shop to buy some cakes and as we were heading back we noticed this shop for sale. I had always fancied having my own business, because it would mean that I could spend more time with the family. I was heavily pregnant at the time and there was a distinct possibility my husband might be made redundant the following year, so the thought of working for ourselves greatly appealed. Anyway we left it at that. Then three weeks later, we picked up the local newspaper and we saw the shop for sale. It was a bit run down and desperately in need of updating and so we decided to take up the challenge and moved to Newport.

It was a struggle at the beginning because, much to our disappointment, the business was slow for the first two years. We would literally sit by the window and watch people walk straight past the shop. I think at the best of times we were only taking a hundred pound a week to pay for bills, which was not ideal. We had a self-service shop, which made us different from our competitors further down the road. There you had to ask for your goods at the counter and you did not have the option to browse or change your mind, you paid for what you asked for. In our shop people could come in, peruse the aisles, select what they wanted and pay when they were ready. We kept wondering 'What on earth is going on?' and as time went on we suspected the problem might be because of our backgrounds. I suppose it is hard to fit in as an outsider in any market town but if you have a different religion or race it can make it even harder.

We extended our hours and waited patiently in the hope that people would warm to us. Slowly but surely people came into the shop and as our reputation grew so did the number of customers. It was a wonderful feeling to come on a Sunday and see a queue of people waiting outside. We had regular customers that became good friends. As time went on we were able to extend our business and property. I raised all of my three children there and I have wonderful memories of helping out at the local school and feeling part of the community. We have since moved away and sold the shop, but I have some happy memories of living in Newport.

Equal Treatment:
A Ugandan Asian's reflection on working as a multi-lingual health care professional in Shropshire by Pal Virdee.

Pal Virdee left Narobi, Kenya to come to England in 1966 and lived in Yorkshire before moving to Shropshire in 1974. She has been working as a qualified health professional for the past forty-three years.

Growing up, my parents had very strong ideas about keeping our culture and identity as Sikhs. They used to say, 'If you lose your identity, that's it, you're gone' and I have kept that advice ever since. I raised both of my children to speak Punjabi and I did not speak a word of English with them until they were older. I remember once I spoke to the milkman and I think that is the first time my son realised I could speak English. He looked at me in astonishment and said 'I didn't know you could speak English Mum', which shows you can't keep secrets from your kids for too long [laughs]. Even though I raised my children to speak Punjabi, they have picked up English quickly and by the age of three they could speak both languages fluently and have gone on to do very well. I am really proud of them. They say their morning prayers and eat their Indian food, which is a change from their teenage years when they only ate English food. I have always cooked Indian food because this is the diet I was brought up with in Kenya and it suits me best.

I think it is a shame that so many Asian children are growing up without any knowledge of their heritage or language because these skills can help many of the older people in the community. When I first came to Shropshire, I was the only Asian midwife who spoke multiple languages and it was useful because I could make a difference. I made tapes in Hindi and Punjabi to teach Indian women about how to bathe children so that they do not get any infections. In those days, Asian women used to dunk the child in the bath and put water on them from head to toe without realising that it could cause eye infections or other problems. This is probably what they did in India, Pakistan and Bangladesh, so it was good for them to learn how to wash the baby's face first and then put the baby in the bath water slowly.

I have always struggled with professionals that think you can only give medical advice in English or by body language. There are so many misunderstandings that can happen. This is why I am committed to interpreting and helping people of all backgrounds to have equal access to services. It is about giving everyone the equal treatment they deserve. I hope after my forty-three years of service this will be the legacy that I have left behind.

Taking the Heat off the Situation:
A Bangladeshi restaurant worker's experiences in Shrewsbury by Sufu Amir.

Sufu Amir came to Wellington in 1965 to join his Uncle who had been living and working in Shropshire. Sufu now lives in Oswestry with his family and runs his own business.

My first job was at an Indian restaurant in Shrewsbury, at the age of fourteen and a half. I had been in England for only two years then and so I barely knew any English. I had been going to school prior to this, but I made a decision to leave in order to help my uncle meet the financial needs of his family here and back home in Bangladesh.

As you can imagine, Indian restaurants were few and far between then. In those days restaurants and pubs would serve drinks until half-ten and at weekends around half-eleven. So come half-ten, half-eleven every night the restaurant would be full with people eating and drinking and occasionally we would have the odd person who had drunk too much and that is when trouble would start. I remember one night, a few other waiters and I were physically picked up and taken outside of the restaurant as if to say 'This is our place and you don't belong here'. It was not unusual to have this type of abuse in those days; we were always being reminded that we did not belong here or that we did not fit in. I never retaliated though, because that can only aggravate the problem. So instead I would make a joke to take the heat from the situation and sometimes it worked. I made them laugh so much that they would take me by the shoulder and say 'Sorry mate I didn't mean it' and that would be the end of that. I am pleased to say, we do not get much abuse anymore, which is very reassuring.

I think when people get to know you, it can change how they feel. When I first came to Oswestry to open my restaurant, I was greeted with a beautiful bouquet of flowers which really helped me to feel welcome and inspired me to want to know the community and be part of it. And I do feel part of the community, I have lived there, my children have studied there and have all gone on to be successful.

Part 5
Community and Voluntary Work

In this section, we learn some ways in which arrivals in Shropshire have strengthened their confidence by joining a range of community activities. We see how family relationships and values provide a compass to guide young people, how a particular group can build its own networks for support and how some of those telling their stories have become important figures in their wider communities – through churches and various voluntary organisations.

Setting up Community Support Networks:
A Ghanaian story by Olivia Somuah.

Olivia Somuah was born in Ghana and came to England in 1989. She lived in London before moving to Shropshire to join her son in 2003. Here Olivia describes her work with the Telford African Welfare Association, which she helped develop in 2003.

We started the Telford African Welfare Association because we felt that there was a need to raise awareness about the needs and issues affecting the African community. Many of them had difficulty accessing services because of the language barrier or other issues and so we provide advice to services on how to meet their needs.

We started the association here in my house. Everyday my house was always busy with activity. I had people staying for days and even months whilst they looked for work and accommodation. If you had come to my house at anytime, you would find people sleeping in my living room or my second bedroom, just so that they could have a place to stay. The Africans called me 'Mum' because that is what I was for many of them; I took care of them or provided guidance in the way my grandmother did in Africa.

My involvement in the association was very much inspired by time in Broadwater Farm[4] in London, an area that is notorious for crime and gangs. I was involved in a steering committee that helped deliver consultation about different issues affecting the lives of local residents and we helped set up support groups. It shows how by coming together as a community you can make big changes. I decided to go on and study in Health and Social Care because it always helps to be knowledgeable about the issues you are championing.

I feel very blessed that at the age of fifty-two I am able to do all that I do, although I think my greatest achievement is my granddaughters Chloe and Emma. They have mixed English and African heritage and they are my angels, they make everything I do worthwhile.

---

[4] Broadwater Farm housing estate in Tottenham, North London was the scene of major race riots in October 1985.

The Family:
A Bangladeshi opinion on family and community by Torikot Ullah.

Torikot Ullah left Bangladesh at the age of eleven in 1970 and moved to Shrewsbury to set up his family business in 1981.

I had a good life in Shropshire to be honest. I have never really had any real problems since I have been here. I had visited Shrewsbury a few times before I decided to live here and I thought this would be a nice place to raise my children. I had been living in London before then, working in the family business and I was ready to get away from the busy city life.

When I came to Shrewsbury there was only a small Bangladeshi community and so, in the first two years I was here, I went around to each and every Bangladeshi home. We had a lot in common because most of us were trying to set up our own businesses and we were able to support each other and offer advice. We set up the Shropshire Bangladeshi Welfare Association for all new families moving to the county, to provide support, organise cultural events and deliver fundraising for different charities.

The support aspect is a very important part of my culture because family and friendships offer a safety net until people are strong enough to branch out on their own. When I came here I worked in the family business along with cousins and extended relatives. In my culture, success is not for the individual but for the whole family and community. Nowadays, our children do not feel the same way because they have different opportunities. My own children have not ventured into the family business and are preparing to be mainstream professionals. My eldest son has recently finished his Masters in Cancer Research and my youngest son is studying Medicine at Leicester University. I'm very happy for them and I wish them well, but I think their future lies outside of Shropshire, where there are more opportunities available for them.

Making a Contribution:
A Jamaican's thoughts on rural life and the importance of becoming part of the community
by Leon Murray.

Leon Murray came to Wellington, Shropshire in 1962. He worked for GKN Sankey and is now semi-retired and is involved in the Methodist Church alongside his work as a Magistrate in Telford. Leon Murray recently received an MBE for his work in Community and Race relations.

It was easier for me to fit in than most, because Jamaica has many cultural similarities to Britain. We eat similar food from roast beef and Yorkshire pudding and we speak the same language and had the same currency, which in my time was a pound, shilling and pence. We even share a common ancestry that many people do not realise. My own father was half Scottish and he would tell us stories about the UK and at school we learnt about England and so we had a good grounding of the country before we came here.

I was raised in a farm in a small rural community and so when I came to Shropshire I could easily empathise with Shropshire life. I know how isolating rural life can be and how it feels not to have access to a taxi at a moments notice or to have everything you need in a local shop. I also know how small communities view outsiders and how difficult it can be to gain acceptance, whatever background you are from. When I first came here, people did not know what to expect from me because they had never been around different types of people before. I was the first black member of the Methodist Youth Fellowship and I remember some of the older congregation did not know how to take me, or felt suspicious perhaps because they thought I would not stay for long. But I did stay and I made some wonderful friendships that I still have to this very day.

I think my role in the church and my voluntary work really helped pave the way for making friendships and earning people's trust and respect. Back then, people did not realise that immigrant communities had skills and that they could make important contributions to the community or to the economy. I found as I took on more responsibilities and proved I had something to offer it helped open up further opportunities. Shropshire has a lot to offer people of all backgrounds, which is why I strongly encourage people to get involved in the community and support local farms and shops.

Family Values:
A Jamaican story of the relationship between father and son
by Verley Brissett.

Verley Brissett was born in Jamaica in 1949 and came to England to join his parents in Wolverhampton in 1970. He moved to Shropshire in 1995 and works as a Youth Development Officer, in addition to his work with the West Indian Association Steel Band and the Telford and Wrekin Race Equality Partnership.

I had one incident with the police and my father soon got me back on the straight and narrow. I remember sitting in a car with my friends on one of our famous nights out to Leeds, without a provisional licence and L plates. It was a yellow Austin Cambridge and I was sitting at the back all excited, until out of nowhere we went straight into this three wheeled Robin Reliant turning both right over, with wheels spinning in the air. We panicked, got out of the car and ran away as fast as we could, without realising we had left identification in the car. Inevitably we were caught and taken to the Police Station and foolishly, gave false statements thinking we could get away with it.

I remember going home to tell my father about what I had done. That very same day he marched me back to the Police Station to confess. The Police Sergeant took me by the arm, stood me by a police cell and said 'I have a good mind to lock you up', although luckily he didn't. My provisional licence was suspended for a year and I was fined for a hefty amount, even though I had been sitting in the backseat. The worst thing was seeing my father's disappointment because up to that point I had never been in trouble in my life. My father said 'if you had been sent to prison, I would have disowned you' and I believed him because my father was an honest man and he only wanted the best for us.

My father is a strong character in my life. I remember a number of incidents were he intervened and stopped me from making bad decisions. I honestly believe my father helped make me into the man I am today. When I was very young, my father would only have to shout us once and I would be there. If I was around older people I would have to refer to them as 'Mr' and 'Mrs' and I knew how to be respectful. If I ever stepped out of line there was only one place that I could hide and that is at my Auntie's house and mind you, she is six foot tall and she could give any grown man a good hidin'. All of the work that I do today is about helping our youngsters to reconnect to the values I was raised with in Jamaica and to give them a firm grounding to overcome challenges in their lives.

Verley Brissett with his daughter

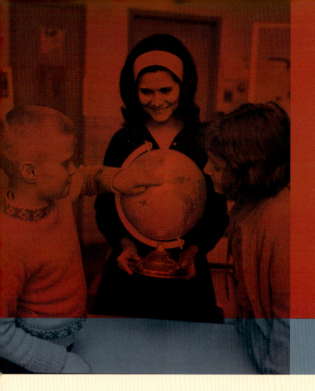

Part 6
Becoming Part of the Community

Getting to know the neighbours and making new friends can help people to settle in and to learn about and become part of Shropshire life. The accounts shared in this section help us to learn about the challenges and opportunities facing individuals and groups as they settle into the county. We have already seen how some of the activities mentioned in Part 6 also help people to settle into their Shropshire environment. Children may make a bridge between the "old country" and the new; and schools offer opportunities for the younger generation to learn about the ways of life of the various ethnic groups in Shropshire.

The accounts given here mostly seem to show a good spirit on both sides. The incomers have been ready to take the risk of seeking out friendship and Salopians appear to have been ready to offer friendship. Perhaps this is an advantage of settling in smaller places, rather than big and alienating cities.

When We Came:
A Jamaican experience of living in Hadley in the 60s and a reflection on changing times by Merle Taylor.

Merle Taylor came to live in Hadley Shropshire in 1969 to join her fiancé, now her husband. Here Merle talks about her early life living in Hadley and how it is different today.

It is difficult to parallel what we had been through to many of the newcomers because we had the advantage of knowing the language and the culture and also times were different then.

When I came here, Hadley was a small and vibrant community. There used to be a furniture shop on the corner and a post office and a grocery shop that would deliver to your door. You have to remember that was a big thing in those days, because not many people had cars and so we relied on our local shops. We had a dress shop, shoe shop and lots of other stores and we could go into Wellington for anything that you wanted. We used to take our children down to the shoe shop and they would have their feet measured and buy new shoes and the service was wonderful.

People used to be friendly; when you passed people in the street they would always say 'Good morning' or 'Good afternoon' and you could always strike up conversation, which almost always started with the weather. I remember when we first had our house, we had neighbours who we would stop and talk to as we went about our everyday business, such as hanging out the terry towel nappies on the washing line because in those days people did not have disposable nappies or washing machines. It was nice having a little chat and catch up because there was so much to talk about, whether it is about the family, work or music. We did not struggle to find work because jobs were plentiful then. Most people worked at GKN Sankeys, although I worked as a nurse for a short period of time, because that is what I trained to be in Jamaica.

I think the lives of my children have been enriched by coming to this country. All of my children have a good standard of education; they all have degrees and are loving and respectful. And I am pleased with my life here; I would not live anywhere else.

A Slower Pace of Life:
A Chilean perspective on fitting into Shrewsbury and feeling part of the community by Alicia Randall.

Alicia Randall was born in Chile in 1934 and has travelled and lived in Germany with her English husband, who was then a staff member of the Naval Army Air Force Institute. Here Alicia talks about her experience of moving to Shrewsbury in 1969.

When I first came to Shrewsbury, life felt very slow because I had been so used to having an active life, you know juggling work, family life and housework; my life was like a wheel turning all the time. I used to go to the theatre, ballet or different cultural activities and so when I came here I found it boring. The pace of life was so slow and there was nothing to do and I remember saying to my husband, 'I cannot stay at home all of the time doing housework, I have to work or do something'. After ten months I decided to volunteer at the local hospital working at the care home for older people. At first I was worried that I did not have enough experience but I soon got into the swing of things. After a few months I was employed full time and I worked there for eighteen years before I retired.

It is the people I met that helped me to settle. Before I came here, I heard that Shropshire people are snobby and unfriendly, but I did not find that. The first day I came here, I had three well wisher cards and a plant on the door step, which was wonderful. A lot of our neighbours go to church, which perhaps makes them friendlier then most although you can never generalise. I have good friends here and through various contacts I have been able to meet lots of different people including other South Americans, which is nice.

Keeping the Connection:
An El Salvadorian's view on raising mixed heritage children in Shropshire
by Consuela Avila.

Consuela Avila was born in El Salvador in 1935 and left when she married her English husband. Consuela came to Shropshire in 1967 and worked as a Spanish teacher in various schools around Shropshire, before recently retiring.

I feel very settled here in Shrewsbury and I have generally not encountered any problems. I used to go around schools and teach people about my culture, which I sometimes miss from time to time. It was rewarding to go into schools because the children were receptive to my culture and wanted to know more about my country and where I came from. When I have the opportunity I watch Spanish films and meet up with other Spanish speaking people. Sometimes it is nice to keep the connection to my heritage.

I am aware that I have a very strong South American accent but as a lady once told me, if one has culture, people will find a way of understanding you. I will give you an example. I had been living in England for over a year or so and I went to the butcher's to buy some turkey. When I arrived the shop was very crowded but nonetheless I queued patiently and when it came to my turn to be served I asked politely for half a pound of turkey. The butcher looked at me bemused before turning to the other customers and gesturing for help, as though he could not understand a word I was saying. I replied "You know turkey… as in what people eat at Christmas" and sure enough, everyone in the shop roared with laughter. Sometimes people think if you have an accent you are ignorant but this is not the case.

Adapting to British Parenting Styles:
A Ghanaian contrasts them with his home culture by Zaglago Light.

Zaglago Light was born in Ghana in 1977 and moved to Shropshire in 2003, with his family. Here Zaglago talks how he has adapted to the different parenting culture in the UK.

I do not even know my neighbours' name and perhaps, once in a while if I see them I will raise my hand and say 'Hello' but that is not the same as in Ghana. In Ghana everybody's home is open to you and people know each other by name. I was brought up in a community where everyone in your family and community has a role in your life. Even if they are your aunts or uncles they all have a right to guide you and even discipline you if need be. If I saw young girls smoking in the street I could tell them off and their parents would not mind. Over here you cannot do that.

My own son was born here in Shropshire and so I have adapted to the parenting culture here. It is difficult because most of us work long hours and so we cannot spend much time with our children and we do not have the support of extended family nearby. When we are at work, we put our son into day-care which is unheard of in Ghana. Everyday my son is exposed to ideas and influences outside of his family life. Occasionally I will hear him say 'Oh dear' or use English words that are not part of my day-to-day vocabulary, which is fine but I would also like him to learn his own language too so he can keep connected to his family heritage.

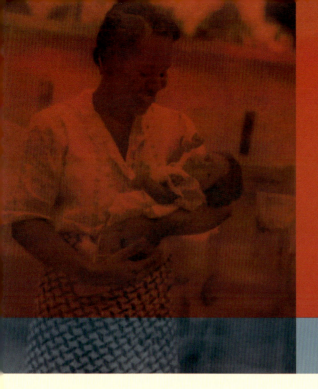

Part 7
Future Hopes and Challenges

All of us have different ideas about what is important for future generations. This is only natural given we have different experiences, values and outlooks. Sometimes we may find that our outlook changes with time. Perhaps we worry more for our children if we are parents or for older people when we have sick parents and relatives.

The accounts in the next section provide an insight into the future hopes and challenges shared by people from different backgrounds. Their insights enable us to understand more about the challenges and opportunities facing new and current generations in the county.

Feeling Settled:
A Japanese perspective on the differences between life in Japan and life in Shropshire by Takeshi Kawai.

Takeshi Kawai was born in Osaka in Japan in 1974 and came to Shropshire in 1998 where he is now settled and runs his own business.

I am probably one of the few people that have stayed on here in Telford. Most Japanese people stay here for a few months or years and return home, depending on the length of their employment contract. My experience is slightly different to most because I had lived in England before.

I first came to England as a tourist. I came because I like British culture; it feels familiar to me. The first thing I did when I came is visit several motorbike and car museums. I then decided to return to England to study English language at Sussex University, which was a real eye-opener for me because I had never been around people from different backgrounds. In Japan you very rarely meet foreigners so it was very exciting to be around people with different accents, views and experiences. I lived there for a while, mainly organising study placements for other Japanese students whilst travelling around the country and that is when I decided to make Britain my home.

I came to Telford because there are many Japanese factories here. I arrived by train and to be honest I did not have a good first impression. When we passed the run-down factories in Wolverhampton I thought 'Oh dear, what have I done?', but when I got into Telford Central I was relieved that this area is much nicer.

I still have contact with my friends in Japan and sometimes whilst talking to them I realise how greatly my life has changed. Perhaps if I had been living in Japan I would have been working for a corporate firm from nine to nine or commuting to the city for an hour on a busy packed train [laughs]. But now my life is very different and much more relaxed. My wife and I have our own business and this is the ideal place to be, with lots of nature around.

A Better Standard of Living:
An Indian contemplates the changing quality of life in India and in Britain after spending forty years living here by Rashpal Singh.

Rashpal Singh came to live in Shropshire in 1974 with his family and worked for GKN Sankey before moving into the finance industry. Rashpal Singh is now semi-retired and works as a magistrate in Telford.

When I came to this country my average wage was about ten pounds a week and even with a bit of overtime we earned thirty-two pounds a week. Hardly any of the houses had carpets and the toilets were in separate outhouses in the garden. We never predicted that one day we would be sitting in nice houses like this or have the time to do voluntary work for the community, which shows how the standard of living has improved for everyone, no matter who they are or where they come from.

The same applies to India. Every time I go back I am astounded by how life has improved. It sometimes feels as though you have come to a foreign country. People have bikes, cars and motorbikes and TVs which I did not have growing up. Even among the very poor there are people working hard and making the most of the opportunities available to them. When I go back it can be difficult to adjust because things are not quite as how you remembered them, but with time you soon get into the swing of things. I think for the next generation they will never know India the way I knew it, which is inevitable because nothing stays the same.

Open Spaces and Friendly Faces:
A Taiwanese view of life in Shropshire and on education in Taiwan and Shropshire by Mary Lu.

Mary Lu worked at a University in Taiwan teaching Mandarin to foreign students and left to come to England in 1982. Here Mary Lu talks about the difference in education and the reason why she has chosen to raise her children in Shropshire.

To most Chinese parents, education is very important and most parents would expect their children to go onto university and get a masters or PhD. Schooling is very competitive and it is not unusual for parents to supervise their child's homework and to make sure that they get good grades. I remember when I used to go to high school in Taipei I had to study through the night to prepare for my exams. It was like that for all of us. We suffered from sleep deprivation because we had endless exams every day. You can never get a break because even over the summer you would have to take extra classes.

When my niece was taking her secondary school exams, she used to get up at six and come from school at ten because she would have to stay and take extra classes in the subject areas she is weaker in. By the time she had come home and finished her homework she would not actually go to bed until eleven-thirty and as you can imagine she was exhausted. I took my own children back briefly a few years ago, but they soon came back because they could not adjust to the demands at school.

I think England offers a better quality of life then in China. My children enjoy school here and have a balance of recreational and academic activities. In Bridgnorth where we live, we have lots of open spaces for them to play and enjoy themselves; it is a good place to live.

Mary Lu's children enjoying the snow in their first year in England.

They Call Us Dirty Gypsies:
A Romany perspective on stereotypes and misconceptions about Traveller/Gypsy people by Julie Brown.

Julie Brown[5] was born in Shrewsbury in 1946 and has travelled around many parts of the county before settling in Lawley Traveller Site with her family 1973.

Water cans used by Travellers in early times as a safe and hygienic way of cleaning away from the living area.

There is so much about us that people don't know. For a start, people call us 'dirty Gypsies', but they don't know how we live or anything about our traditions. Gypsies are very clean people. We have two separate sinks, one for washing up and another for cleaning hands. Before you wash up you have to wash your hands first, it is an unwritten rule that everybody knows whether they are a child or an adult.

We have all the amenities that any other person has, including showers, baths and basins. We keep our toilets separate from the house because we think it is unhygienic to have a toilet near the place where you eat and sleep. I know people hear stories of travellers or gypsies defecating in fields or leaving rubbish but that is not typical. Where there is access to bins and toilets they are used. It is part of culture you see; from a young age, we are taught to take care of the home. So when I was young my youngest sister would stay at home and clean and tidy while the rest of us would go out selling flowers and charms. And when she grew up and had her own family she continued to take care of the home like I did. For the boys it's different because their role is to provide, so my brother used to go out with my father learning his trade.

It has always been this way, although I think with time these traditions will slowly go as we have more and more pressures from the outside. I say this because I have had experiences where I have been evicted from a site for no reason. The worst time was when we were put into a house. My children, grown boys and girls had to share one room; it almost took us to breaking point. People do not realise we do not want to bother other people; we just want to have our own sites where we can live freely. Why shouldn't we practice our culture like everyone else? If we choose to burn our caravans at a funeral, why should we not be able to do that? We burn it out of respect and then after people have mourned we clear up the ashes and debris. These days we have fire brigade interfering or neighbours complaining and so it is making it more and more difficult for us to keep our culture and that saddens me.

[5] Pseudonym changed from Mrs X in the original oral history interview

The Legacy We Will Leave Behind:
A Polish view about the Polish migrants who settled in Shropshire after 1945 by Jadwiga Matecka.

Jadwiga Matecka left Stafford and came to Wellington, Shropshire in 1965 to join her husband who was working for GKN Sankey. Here Jadwiga talks about the legacy she hopes the established Polish community will leave behind.

I think hard work will be the legacy we will leave behind, not only my family but other Polish families that have come here after the War. Whatever challenges we have faced in life, we have overcome them and this comes from our strength of character. If I told you some of the things I have been through in my life you probably would not believe me because they are truly horrific. I have seen people literally dying of hunger before my very eyes and I have experienced such intense hunger that I have literally eaten scraps of bread from the floor.

It would be hard for people to believe how we lived even here in England. When I came to Reading, the army barracks we were put into were no different to the labour camps we had left in Siberia. All the families that came here were separated, men in one barrack and women in the other. We had beds lined up against the wall, like a hospital. All of our food was rationed. We used to travel on buses to work at five o'clock in the morning and come home at eight o'clock at night. If we missed the bus or came home late, the canteen would be closed and we would not eat, it was quite simple.

I think experiencing these types of hardships make you stronger and help you appreciate what you have in life. Even now in my life I never throw food away because I know what it is like to be hungry and I never want to be hungry again. I feel grateful my children will never have to experience what I have been through.

Fading Identity:
A Northern Irish perspective on identity and belonging by Ann Baxendale.

Ann Baxendale was born in Belfast in 1960 and came to Shropshire in 1991 in connection with her husband's work in the British Army before finally settling in the county in 2000. Ann Baxendale now works for the Telford and Wrekin Council as an Internal Communications Advisor.

I suppose, in Northern Ireland young people had to be politically aware, they had no choice; it was their only way of staying safe. When I was growing up there I had no sense of the danger. I had a normal upbringing with my family in Lisburn, with my cousins nearby and we did normal family things such as going on holiday and so on. We lived in a nice neighbourhood, where the families knew each other and I have happy memories of playing in the street until the late hours. Occasionally we would have the odd sign that would indicate the troubles are getting closer, such as a bomb going off at night. That is when my parents made the decision to bring us over to England.

At first it was very difficult for us because we moved to Oldham in an area called Limeside and it was a big council estate. I remember feeling embarrassed to bring my friends back home because I just did not want people to know where I lived even though my home was clean and lovely and perfectly welcoming. My mother worked all the hours she could at a local catalogue firm so we could afford to buy a house and soon enough we had moved to a much nicer area. People knew that we had come to escape the troubles and there were several instances at school where the name calling got quite bad and children would say 'Take your troubles home'. I could not tell my parents at the time because of course, I did not want to trouble them. Moving here had been traumatic enough.

As time went on and I settled in, I didn't feel as though I stood out so much and as my accent faded so did many of my connections to Ireland. I remember going back to Northern Ireland as a teenager and realising how much my life had changed. Everywhere you went you were stopped and searched as you went in and out of supermarkets. I feel as though I had a lot more freedom to grow up in England without having to worry about politics or religion.

I suppose that is one of the nice things about living in Shropshire as well. There are lots of different cultures here and people are able to live their own life without interference from others and in my view that can only be a good thing.

Bridges – making global connections

Bridges is
- a centre for global education based in Shropshire
- working to raise awareness of global issues and diversity through understanding connections between people and places
- aiming to empower people to take action to build a better world

Bridges works with
- formal and informal education organisations such as schools, colleges and community groups
- groups and individuals with global connections or an interest in global issues
- partner groups, volunteers and friends who support our aims.

Bridges offers
- **Training** – Raise awareness of global issues and diversity with your staff by booking in-house training or attending one of our programmed sessions
- **Workshops** – Get your group or class talking about the issues that matter with an active workshop or engaging talk
- **Projects** – Take part in one of our long term projects exploring themes such as global citizenship, sustainability and global interdependence.
- **Events** – Share in current work on global issues in your area

To find out more about Bridges
- Visit our website at **www.shropshirebridges.org.uk**
- Call us on **01952 255526**
- Email: **info@shropshirebridges.org.uk**
- Write to Bridges, The Studios, Mansell Road, Wellington, Shropshire TF1 1QQ

'Views from Shropshire' is a Heritage Lottery funded project collecting oral histories from first generation immigrants who have settled in Shropshire from different parts of the world. The aim of the project is to help raise awareness of Shropshire's multi-cultural heritage and to create a dialogue for different communities to communicate to each other based on their common values and experiences.

Sixty-eight participants from diverse communities took part in one-to-one interviews and reminiscence workshops. Participants included people from Africa, Asia, Europe, South America and the West Indies.

This project has:

- Archived thirty oral history transcripts at Shropshire Archives

- developed a book and schools resource for key stage two and three, in consultation with teachers and curriculum advisors in Shropshire.

- developed a short community film and educational resource which has been used in diversity training for community groups and organisations.

- delivered workshops with youth and community groups exploring issues around 'diversity', 'identity' and 'community'', which were displayed at the 'Views from Shropshire' exhibition which took place in October 2008.

To find out more about this project please contact
info@shropshirebridges.org.uk

Snapshots from the Views from Shropshire Reminiscence Workshops